A Spirituality of Homecoming

Henri J. M. Nouwen

John S. Mogabgab, *Series Editor*

UPPER
ROOM BOOKS®

NASHVILLE

THE HENRI NOUWEN SPIRITUALITY SERIES
A Spirituality of Homecoming
Copyright © 2012 The Henri Nouwen Legacy Trust.
All rights reserved.

The Upper Room Web site: www.upperroom.org.
The Henri Nouwen Society Web site: www.HenriNouwen.org.

UPPER ROOM®, UPPER ROOM BOOKS®, and design logos are trademarks owned by The Upper Room®, a ministry of GBOD®, Nashville, Tennessee. All rights reserved.

Unless otherwise indicated, Scripture quotations are from *The New Jerusalem Bible*, copyright © 1985 by Darton, Longman & Todd, Ltd. and Doubleday, a division of Random House, Inc. Reprinted by permission.

Scripture quotations designated JB are taken from *The Jerusalem Bible*, copyright © 1966 by Darton, Longman & Todd, Ltd. and Doubleday, a division of Bantam Doubleday Dell Publishing Group, Inc. Reprinted by permission.

Scripture quotations designated NRSV are taken from the *New Revised Standard Version Bible*, copyright © 1989, Division of Christian Education of the National Council of Churches of Christ in the United States of America. Used by permission. All rights reserved.

Cover and Interior Design: Sue Smith and Pearson & Co. Cover art: Gogh, Vincent van (1888). *Mas at Saintes Maries de la Mer*. Private Collection/Art Resource, NY. Photo on page 62 by Mary Ellen Kronstein. Used by permission.

Library of Congress Cataloging-in-Publication Data
Nouwen, Henri J. M.
A spirituality of homecoming / by Henri J. M. Nouwen.
    p. cm. — (The Henri Nouwen spirituality series)
  Includes bibliographical references.
  ISBN 978-0-8358-1114-9
1. Spiritual life—Catholic Church. I. Title.
BX2350.3.N6924 2013
248.4'82—dc23

                                                              2012027334

Printed in the United States of America

CONTENTS

About the Henri Nouwen Spirituality Series *iv*

Preface *v*

Acknowledgments *x*

Home in the Heart 12

The Invitation 15

The Call 22

The Challenge 30

The Cost 38

The Reward 47

The Promise 51

Hidden Work 57

Notes 60

Henri J. M. Nouwen's Works Cited 61

About Henri J. M. Nouwen 62

ABOUT THE HENRI NOUWEN SPIRITUALITY SERIES

Henri Nouwen sought the center of things. Never content to observe life from the sidelines, his approach to new experiences and relationships was full throttle. He looked at the world with the enthusiastic anticipation of a child, convinced that right in the midst of life he would find the God who loves us without conditions. Helping us recognize this God in the very fabric of our lives was the enduring passion of Henri's life and ministry.

The Henri Nouwen Spirituality Series embodies Henri's legacy of compassionate engagement with contemporary issues and concerns. Developed through a partnership between the Henri Nouwen Society and Upper Room Ministries, the Series offers fresh presentations of themes close to Henri's heart. We hope each volume will help you discover that in your daily round God is closer than you think.

PREFACE

HENRI NOUWEN often wrote about moving beyond fear. I remember well the first time my husband Geoff and I met Henri. We felt a bit shy as he welcomed us into his Honda Civic, but as he started to drive our fear was swiftly transformed—to terror! Henri's active, expressive hands were rarely on the wheel, and he wanted eye contact as we chatted. I would have preferred him to have eye contact with the road. This was not our unique experience: a couple of years earlier Henri had famously totaled a new car within blocks of the dealership.

On that day with Henri we moved from fear to terror, then from terror to pizza. Henri happily introduced us to his favorite pizza restaurant, where the wait staff knew him by name. He made us feel at home with him, sharing very personally about his own life, his anxieties and fears, and he was deeply interested in our life choices and experiences. He warmly welcomed us into an intimate time together.

In this little book about homecoming, Henri describes the first disciples asking Jesus where he lived, and beginning to get to know him by spending time together. I've often wondered how Henri Nouwen would function in today's world. He would quickly recognize a paradox: the world's suffering, local news, and even personal relationships have all become more immediate with instant global communication, yet also more detached and controlled, represented on a screen. Henri urges his readers to dare unexpected relationships: "If we want to find Jesus, we need to spend time with people who are not the same as we are. And we have to listen to them."

These reflections are adapted from a series of Lenten talks that Henri offered in 1985 in Cambridge, Massachusetts. Henri spoke about following Jesus as a response to an invitation, a response that will lead us home. He explores the fears and wounds that can prevent us from hearing or responding to Jesus' call, and the challenge of incarnating Jesus rather than simply imitating him.

At the time of these talks, Henri had been spending half of his time teaching at Harvard and the other half traveling, speaking to large audiences about the spiritual grounding needed to work for greater justice. This unsettled lifestyle had taken a toll. While former students fondly recall his welcoming home in Cambridge, Henri experienced his interior life as "living in a very dark place." He explains: "I found myself praying poorly, living somewhat isolated from other people, and very much preoccupied with burning issues." Within months of these Lenten talks, Henri would uproot his life, seeking again to respond to Jesus' invitation to "come and see" where he lived. His recognition of L'Arche as a place for his heart was all about home:

When I visited the L'Arche community in France I experienced a sense of at-homeness I had not experienced at Yale, in Latin America, or at Harvard. The noncompetitive life with mentally handicapped people, their gifts of welcoming me regardless of name or prestige, and the persistent invitation to "waste some time" with them opened in me a place that until then had remained unavailable to me, a place where I could hear the gentle invitation of Jesus to dwell with him.[1]

In these pages, Henri articulates the spirituality of someone who follows Jesus and is thus able to find home anywhere and everywhere, discovering joy hidden in being open to the reality of pain. This is a central theme of all Henri's writing: do not be afraid of suffering, whether your own or others'. Henri includes only one personal story, but it is powerful. He describes a time of depression, perhaps because he is feeling overwhelmed by the world's many urgent issues, and he is feeling lonely and needy. Because he is in Flagstaff, he decides to go to the Grand Canyon. Interestingly, he isn't beset with an urge to leap in! Instead, the geologic layers, laid one by one over millennia, become a comforting meta-phor that puts his life into perspective. In that vastness, Henri's discouragement falls away.

A Spirituality of Homecoming is about the moments and choices that allow God to break through our blockages so that we can become free.

Carolyn Whitney-Brown

St. Jerome's University

Waterloo, Ontario

ACKNOWLEDGMENTS

T HE APPEARANCE of this fourth volume in the Henri Nouwen Spirituality Series is due, in no small measure, to the encouragement of my colleagues at Upper Room Books. Jeannie Crawford-Lee, Rita Collett, and Eli Fisher cheered me on as I wrestled transcriptions from the uneven original recordings of Henri's meditations. Designer Nelson Kane has crafted a cover that conveys the spacious invitation contained in these pages. Nathan Ball, Judith Leckie, and Sue Mosteller of The Henri Nouwen Legacy Trust deserve deepest thanks for their penetrating comments on the penultimate draft of this book. Finally, gratitude greater than words can express belongs to Carolyn Whitney-Brown, a former colleague of Henri's at L'Arche Daybreak in Richmond Hill, Ontario. She generously agreed to write the Preface in the midst of last minute preparations for teaching university summer school.

John S. Mogabgab
Series Editor

"Those who love me will keep my word, and my Father will love them, and we will come to them and make our home with them."

(John 14:23, NRSV)

Home in the Heart

You will discover an order
and a familiarity which
deepens your longing
to stay at home.

—*With Open Hands*

THE SPIRITUAL life is a journey to the center, the center in which we come in touch with the pain of God as well as with the love of God, the pain of our world as well as the hope for our world, the pains of our own lives as well as the light that breaks into our darkness. It is a journey in which we resist the many distractions that pull us away from the center with an endless number of things that quite literally "occupy" us. And it is a journey of prayer in which we stand in the presence of God with a listening heart.

Entering into the heart is entering into the kingdom of God.

—The Way of the Heart

The heart means the core of our being. It includes the deep recesses of our psyche, our moods and feelings, our emotions and passions, and also our intuitions, insights, and visions. The heart is the place where we are most human. A listening heart therefore means a heart in which we stand open to God with all we are and have. That is a great act of trust and confidence.

An undistracted life is one in which we want to lead all we see, all we hear, and all we do to the center. Or to say it better, to the heart. It is the ongoing discipline of taking things to heart. But the heart to which we lead all things is not simply our heart. It is God's heart as well. When we take our world to the center, to the heart, we will find that the heart is the place where we meet God. From there all is transformed continuously into the image of him who is the suffering servant of Yahweh.

God is not in the distant heavens or in the hidden depths of the future, but here and now. God has pitched a tent among us. Even more than that, God has made a home in us so that we can make God's home our home.

We find our way home to the heart by following Jesus.[2]

The Invitation

We will see coming to us
the One who has been
waiting for us
from all eternity to
welcome us home.

—*Can You Drink the Cup?*

Come and see.

—John 1:39

"COME AND see" is the invitation Jesus offers two disciples of John the Baptist. How do they respond to that invitation, and how do we?

John the Baptist was a tough man dressed in camel hair, very ascetic. He was a preacher of repentance. With a stern voice he cried out: "You are sinful people! Repent! Repent!"

One day Andrew and another disciple were standing with John when Jesus passed by. The Baptist looked hard at Jesus and said, "Look, there is the lamb of God that takes away the sin of the world" (John 1:29). John knew that the people needed to repent, but he also knew that he could not take away their sins. Taking away sins was not a human possibility. But seeing Jesus, John the Baptist said: "Look, there is the lamb of God that takes away the sin of the world."

John's disciples followed Jesus, who turned around, saw them following him, and said,

"What do you want?" And they said, "Where do you live?" Here, at the beginning of the story, we hear the most important questions: "Where do you live? How is it to be around you?" And Jesus said, "Come and see." How different he was from John the Baptist, who loudly preached "Repent! Repent!" Jesus, this humble servant, this gentle God, just invited John's disciples to come and see where he lived. Jesus invited them in simply to look around, to be there with him. So the disciples went and stayed with him the rest of that day. They became familiar with his place.

Jesus is the host who wants to gather us around the table, the Good Shepherd who invites his people to a table where the cup is overflowing (Ps. 23). This is not a stern, harsh Lord, but the lamb of God who says, "Come into my home." We can read the whole Bible with this image in mind. God is continually inviting us to dwell in the house of the Lord all the days of our life (Ps. 27:4). The Lord wants to be our home. That is why John says that the Word became flesh and pitched a tent among us (see John 1:14). God built a home among us so we could see how much God wants us to be at home with God. "Come and see."

John's Gospel develops this image, and so we find Jesus saying: "Make your home in me, as I have made my home in you" (see John 15:4). Jesus came to make *us* into his home and to invite us to dwell in his house. Suddenly all those biblical images of God's hospitality come together and we realize that *we* are God's home and that we are invited to make our home where God has made God's own home. Our bodies, our hands, our face, our heart are becoming the place where we and God can dwell together in freedom.

God wants us home.

—The Road to Daybreak

This image of "home" continues to expand when Jesus says that he is going to his Father's house to prepare a room and a place at the table for us. In that mansion there is a banquet where the cup overflows and life will be one great celebration of joy with God. I hope we can begin to sense the profundity of this invitation: "Come and see."

What is our response to this invitation? There are three simple words that describe it: *listen, ask,* and *dwell.*

LISTEN

John the Baptist's disciples probably would not have noticed Jesus or followed him if John had not said, "Look, there is the lamb of God." We do not find Jesus on our own, it seems. Someone else points to him. And sometimes we need to really listen because the people who point to Jesus may not be exciting, attractive, or compatible people. We may have certain opinions about them. But we need to listen to them even if we are not comfortable with them because they are too poor or too rich, have a strange accent, dress differently, or speak another language. If we want to find Jesus, we need to spend time with people who are not the same as we are. And we have to listen to them.

ASK

Then we have to ask: "Where do you live?" It is important that we want to know who Jesus is, that we seek him and want to be with him. We need to keep saying, "Lord, I'm not sure I want to follow you. I've heard all sorts of things about you. Show me your place so I can be there and see for myself. I want to get to know you." This is where our prayer begins. Jesus wants that. He wants to call us friends rather than servants and wants us to know everything that he knows, everything that he has heard from his Father (John 15:15). We need to pray for that intimacy. We should not be timid about asking for it.

DWELL

The third part of our response is to dwell. John's disciples stayed with Jesus until four o'clock in the afternoon. We have to dwell with Jesus, listen to him, and get to know him. If we want to be his disciples, we need to be willing to say, "This half hour I want to spend with you, Lord. I am very busy and have many things to do, but I believe that you love me and want to spend time with me." Be with Jesus. Be quiet. Listen to the one who invites you to his home. Gradually, we will notice that we are in his house not only for that half hour, but also throughout the day. We will discover that we are in the house of the Lord wherever we are and whatever we do. By dwelling with the Lord in prayer, we can live in a hostile, violent, competitive world and be at home.

Prayer is the most concrete way to make our home in God.

—Lifesigns

The Call

To follow Jesus is
to participate in the ongoing
self-revelation of God.

—*Compassion*

Follow me.

—Luke 5:27

THE SPIRITUAL journey is essentially different from engaging in hero worship or
joining a therapeutic movement. These forms of
following are typically centered on "me." In hero
worship, we may be looking for a vicarious self
by losing our identity in that of the hero. In many
therapeutic movements, we may be searching for
inner harmony or healing. When Jesus says, "Follow me," he is calling us to let go of "*me*" and to
gradually say, "*You*, Lord, are the one." Jesus calls
us to leave our "me" world, trusting that being at
home in God we will discover who we truly are.

FROM THE LOGIC OF FEAR TO THE
LOGIC OF LOVE

We see the direction of this journey emerging
in the story of Jesus meeting Simon, James, and
John as they were coming in from a night of fishing on Lake Gennesaret (Luke 5:1-11). Crowds

of people eager to hear God's word pressed so close to Jesus that he needed to get into Simon's boat and move away from shore to address them.

Jesus was preaching about the kingdom of God, a kingdom in which everything is turned upside down. Blessed are those whom society considers marginal or not respectable. Something new was happening because the kingdom was close at hand.

When Jesus finished his sermon, Simon said, "Well that was an interesting sermon. Now let's go back to what we were doing before." But when Jesus told Simon and the others to throw out their nets for a catch, Jesus did not return to their normal, day-to-day living as it was before he began his sermon. He wanted now to move beyond the old way of being to the new way of being. But they were talking (as we do) just as they did before. "Listen, Jesus, you are not a fisherman. You don't know what fishing is about. You're a preacher. If we didn't catch anything during the night, we're not going to catch anything during the day! It doesn't make any sense to throw the nets now." And then with a kind of resignation they said, "Well, if you say so, okay. We'll do it."

The disciples' response expresses normal logic. We see this again and again. Remember the big crowd, five loaves, and two fish (Matt. 14:15-21)? Jesus said, "Give them something to eat." The disciples responded, "Lord, five loaves, two fish, big crowd? It doesn't fit." Jesus said, "Give them something to eat." And he said, "Throw out your nets." They did and caught fish, but not just as many as they needed. They caught so many their nets could not hold all the fish. It is the same with the crowd. Jesus didn't just want to be sure that everyone got a little piece of bread. There were twelve big baskets of leftovers! And the boat was so full of fish that Simon didn't know what to do with them.

I am looking. I am listening. Do I see and hear?

—Finding Our Sacred Center

Jesus breaks right through our normal logic. He is moving all of reality to the kingdom.

Suddenly these fishermen were no longer living in the logic of the world. They had entered the logic of God's house, which is beyond all human logic. They had entered a whole new world.

Then Jesus said, "Follow me. Don't be afraid. I will make you catch people. I will introduce you to a whole new way of living." So they left everything and followed him. This scene is important because they indeed left everything behind. We constantly try to hold onto our old logic and Jesus keeps trying to break through it to a new way of being. We are afraid of letting this happen because when we let Jesus enter the center of our lives, our hearts, we will not have control anymore. Maybe we will not have enough to survive in this harsh world. What Jesus keeps promising are realities that we cannot grasp because they are concerned with eternal life. His miracles are signs of that life. Jesus says to us, "Do you remember how

Jesus is living in your heart and offering you all you need.

—The Inner Voice of Love

much bread was left over? Do you remember the catch of fish? How can I make you trust me, make you believe that with me you will not lack anything?" Again and again, when Jesus appears there is more than we need. The Lord is a Lord of abundance who calls us into the kingdom of freedom, peace, joy—that is what finally made the disciples believe, leave their nets, and follow Jesus to their true home.

AWAY FROM THE "ME" WORLD

What about us? Our response to the call is to take small steps away from "me" toward the Lord. Following does not immediately require a dramatic move. How often people ask big questions when they know the small answers! "Do I have to give everything away and go on an overseas mission?" No, it only takes a little step. Be kinder to the people who irritate us. The secret of the spiritual life is that the person who is in touch with the Lord knows what the little steps are. They are small steps of faithfulness, and if we take them in our thinking, our speaking, and our acting, over time they will carry us on a long and possibly dramatic journey. It is a journey in which we hear the call to follow more and more clearly and know where we are going. So let's trust that the steps toward home Jesus asks us to take are very close at hand.

Second, we step away from the world of "mine." Here is the criterion: is our act one of fear for our survival or an act of trust in the call that asks us to move from fear to love? We will know very soon when we act from fear and when we act from love. Always choose love. It is crucial that we not only step away from our fears but that we step *toward* the one who is love, the one who is speaking to us not first of all about hardship and detachment and the cross but about *life*.

We need to keep our eyes on the Lord of abundance. The purpose of all prayer and meditation is to help us keep our eyes on his face. If we want to develop a spiritual life, then we need to keep the Lord in mind and look at him. The spiritual life is not about giving up something but rather about following someone. It is moving toward someone we love. Always stay close to the invitation, "Come and see." If we really *see*, if we really become familiar with the beauty of Jesus and recognize that his beauty is the invitation to love, to go where he calls, then following him will be easy because we are attracted to him. Simon Peter's words will become our own: "We have come to believe and know that you are the Holy One of God" (John 6:69, NRSV).

> *To see Christ is to see God and all of humanity.*
>
> —Behold the Beauty of the Lord

The Challenge

Love is an act of forgiving in
which evil is converted
to good and destruction
into creation.

—*Intimacy*

I say this to you who are listening: Love your enemies, do good to those who hate you, bless those who curse you, pray for those who treat you badly.

—Luke 6:27-28

FOLLOWING JESUS does not mean imitating Jesus, copying his way of doing things. If we imitate someone, we are not developing an intimate relationship with that person. Instead, following Jesus means to give our own unique form, our own unique incarnation, to God's love. To follow Jesus means to live our lives as authentically as he lived his. It means to give away our ego and follow the God of love as Jesus shows us how to do it.

LOVING OUR ENEMIES

Loving our enemies is the core of the Christian message and the challenge that Jesus presents us. If we want to know what Jesus is about, and what following Jesus home is about, then the call to love our enemies is as close to the center as we can get.

Perhaps we have difficulty understanding the call to love enemies because we have a distorted understanding of love. My own life has helped me see that we are needy people. We need attention, affection, influence. These needs are so strong that we may find ourselves arranging our lives in order to satisfy them. But this is a tragic trap because we can never find the attention, influence, or care that really fills our needs. This leads to a life filled with tension as we seek what we cannot find.

Why are we so needy? I think it comes from an awareness of woundedness. We have doubts about our selves. These doubts trace back to deep, early experiences that cause us to feel not fully acceptable as we are. We are not at home with our selves. From our feeling of woundedness we become needy. And in our neediness we wound others. There is an interlocking relationship between needs and wounds that stretches backward and forward from generation to generation. This is the context of what we call "love."

The gospel breaks through this chain of inter-locking needs and wounds. The great message of Jesus is that God loves us first and that we can love one another only because God has loved us first. Jesus calls us to come home to that first love, which precedes all human loves. This is the original blessing, the original acceptance, our orig-inal home. The Christian life means to love one another with God's love and not with the needy, wounded love that can end up harming others.

Only with Jesus can we go to the place where there is nothing but mercy.

—The Road to Daybreak

As we are able to claim God's original love in our innermost self, in our heart, we also begin to see that God loves other people with this same love. When I say to another person, "I love you," it means that meeting that person brings me in touch with the God I am dwell-ing with in the home of my heart. Together we are called to manifest that love. The Christian life is a life of witness to God's original love.

We can see how love of enemies flows directly from this.

Love of enemies is the criterion of holiness. Staretz Silouan, a great twentieth-century spiritual father on Mount Athos, said this: "If you pray for enemies, peace will come to you. And when you love your enemies, take for certain that great divine grace dwells in you."[3] Love of enemies is characteristic of Jesus' life. Even in the midst of his agony on the cross, he could pray, "Father, forgive them; they do not know what they are doing" (Luke 23:34).

Our love for our enemies shows to whom we really belong. It shows our true home.

—Letters to Marc About Jesus

What is an enemy? An enemy is someone we have defined as being against us, in contrast with those who are for us. Many of us have a strange need to divide the world into these two groups. Quite often our identity is dependent on having friends—and having enemies! We define our enemies and they are there to define us.

The good news of the gospel is that God has no enemies. God loves every human being with the same intense love. God is "kind to the ungrateful and the wicked" (Luke 6:35). God "sends down rain to fall on the upright and the wicked alike" (Matt. 5:45). God's love does not make distinctions. If we want to love one another with God's love and not our wounded, needy love, then we are called again and again to make our enemies our friends. Martin Luther King Jr. says: "Love is the only force capable of transforming an enemy into a friend."[4]

BECOMING FREE FROM OUR ENEMIES

Enemies have power over us. We think about them almost constantly and are not free. So love of enemies is a way of becoming free from the enemy. We let them go by starting to love them and to care for them. Our first response to the challenge Jesus puts before us is to pray for our enemies. This is hard. The enemy is an internal presence, so we are dealing here with something very intimate. But if we can go inward to that place where the enemy dwells, then slowly our prayer can convert the anger and worry associated with that hard intimacy. When we do this, we are acting out God's love in our own life.

The second thing we can do is to perform simple acts of service for people with whom we have a hard time. But we must not wait until we feel good about doing something for them. Do it anyway. This is "acting ahead" of our feelings, and that is where healing comes from. Emotions should not decide what we do. Instead, let our knowledge of God's love direct us: *God loves this person as much as God loves me, although it is pretty hard for me to believe it!*

Choose for the truth of what you know.

—The Inner Voice of Love

Small acts of love express our desire for a healed, restored relationship and are independent of whether or not the person likes us. The point is to remind ourselves of the truth that God loves that person as much as God loves us. We can trust that if we act according to our knowledge, then our feelings will catch up. Eventually, we will even discover that our feelings are shaped by our knowledge. This is an important spiritual truth in a world where feelings have become so dominant in our lives.

It is precisely the core of our faith and of our following Jesus that we should be free people, free from the power we give to our enemies so that we can love every human being with a divine love that forgives seventy-seven times again and again (Matt. 18:22).

The Cost

How can wounds
become a source
of healing?

—*The Wounded Healer*

Take up your cross.

—Matt. 11:28-30; 16:24-26; 27:31-38, 45-50

I HAVE SUGGESTED that following Jesus does not mean imitating Jesus. Now I would like to say that following Jesus does not mean being lifted up and away from our struggles. Some people believe that if we have Jesus in our hearts, everything will be wonderful. Jesus is the problem solver and following Jesus is the solution to our problems.

Following Jesus means that we have to keep walking on the ground, keep struggling. The work of living does not necessarily become easier because we are disciples. In fact, discipleship can make life more difficult. At the same time, life becomes radically different. Our struggles and pains become different struggles and pains. The reason for this is that we are no longer living our struggles and pains alone. Following Jesus indeed means that we live our same life, but we live it in companionship with the one who understands us fully—our guide, fellow traveler, the one in whom we can trust our whole life.

The cost of following Jesus is to take up the cross. I want to explore Jesus' cross first. Then I want to speak about our cross, and finally about taking up the cross.

JESUS' CROSS

God created the world through God's Word. All that is has been created by the Word of God. All that is! And that Word of God became flesh. What this means is beautifully expressed by Paul when he says that Jesus Christ, the Word of God, did not cling to his divine privilege of being the one through whom all is created but rather emptied himself and became one of us. More than that, he not only came as one of us, but he was obedient to death, a death on the wood of the cross (Phil. 2:5-8). He wanted to live our life *to the full*, to feel the human condition more profoundly than we ourselves ever could. And he made this visible by dying the most absurd death:

the Holy One nailed naked on a cross between two criminals.

Jesus says, "When I am lifted up from the earth, I shall draw all people to myself" (John 12:32). This means that all humanity—past, present, and future—has been drawn into the mystery of Christ's death and resurrection. It means that in Jesus' death, all human mortality has been embraced. All human suffering is there.

Your cross has been planted in this world as the new sign of hope.

—A Cry for Mercy

OUR CROSS

I want to say something about our cross as a heavy burden. One kind of heavy burden is the cross of the world's suffering, the suffering with which we are bombarded by radio, television, and newspapers. The weight of this suffering can cause us to become passive simply as a survival tactic in the face of so much pain. If we really took all the suffering seriously and personally, we would soon become immobilized. Or we might become angry, because the huge weight of suffering reveals our powerlessness to change things. So we say, "Well, I can't pay attention to all of that. Family and work are enough for me to deal with. I can't deal with all these other problems!"

There is another kind of heavy burden. It concerns not large issues but rather small things, the little irritations that occupy our mind the whole day, like a toothache. It can be a person, a situation, or an unfulfilled hope. These large and small concerns may explain why many of us experience life as an enormous burden and ourselves as overburdened people. When our burdens, our crosses, remain isolated, that is, disconnected from the mystery of God's burden, they become heavier and heavier. A heavy burden is a burden that we have to carry by ourselves.

Jesus says, "Take up your cross and follow me. Take up my burden, which is the burden of the whole world, and it will be a light burden." Here we touch a mystery of the Christian life. It is not that God in Christ came to take away our burdens. God takes us more seriously than that. God came to invite us to connect our burdens with God's burden, our sufferings with God's sufferings. The great invitation of the Christian life is to live a life connected with the Son of God, who died for us, and who wants to give us his burden, which is light because God has carried it for us. Our suffering is still agonizing; but connected with the cross, it becomes one with the suffering of Christ, the suffering that leads us home to a whole new world.

TAKING UP THE CROSS

Taking up the cross does not mean looking for pain or searching for a problem. It means, first of all, acknowledging where we are suffering. We should start with small problems rather than large ones—perhaps someone didn't speak to you today or you didn't get that letter you desired, and it hurts. Seeing and acknowledging small struggles allows us to become at home in our own house, where God dwells. Then we will not be so frightened that something more painful might come along. This is our life. And that means this is also our pain. Let's embrace it, because we will never taste the joy of life if we ignore the pain of life.

FOLLOW ME

The first thing Jesus says is, "Take up your cross." Then he adds, "And follow me! Make it part of your discipleship. Connect it with me. Connect it with God's way." The mystery of prayer is precisely the mystery of an ongoing connectedness with God's suffering in Christ: "Lord, let me bring into your presence my whole being, with all my anger and pain, and let my cross merge with yours. My burden will be your burden, and your burden will fill me with new life and new hope." That is real prayer. Let us bring our whole life into connection with the one who has already suffered it all and lifted it up in his risen body. In

Heart speaks to heart.

—Jesus and Mary

this connection, something new is being born. Renewal is taking place in us. We are finding our way home.

Let me tell you a story about a heavy burden I was carrying. I was feeling depressed about everything. By coincidence, I was in Flagstaff, Arizona, so I decided to go to the Grand Canyon. I saw this multi-million-year-old canyon and its place in an even older creation and thought that if that whole time period were represented by one hour, then I probably was born in a tiny fraction of the last second. Looking at the Grand Canyon, this enormous abyss of beauty, I thought, *My dear, why are you overcome by these problems?* My depression fell away. *In the face of all this, what are you worried about, as if you were carrying the burden of the world? Something has gone on before you and something will go on after you, so why don't you enjoy the brief time you've been given?*

Seeing the Grand Canyon was like seeing a wound in the earth that heals us. That image has stayed with me a long time, because I realized that God is like the Grand Canyon. God suffered a wound, the wound of all humanity, and if I enter into the abyss of divine love, my wound becomes a light burden. I realized that I could acknowledge my wound and not be paralyzed by it, live it and not be consumed by it. In the presence of God's wound, I know myself loved by a love so immense that it leads me home into the very life of our God.

The Reward

Joy is essential to
spiritual life.

—*Here and Now*

I have told you this so that my joy

may be in you and your joy be complete.

—John 15:11. See John 16:20b-22; 15:9b.

THE REWARD of following Jesus is joy. Joyful living is when we are always moving toward something new and are not stuck in the old. Joy is about experiencing life as refreshed and renewed. There is no "old" joy.

JOY AND LOVE

The good news of the gospel is that Jesus wants to give us his joy. The joy Jesus promises is something very different from happiness. Often what people call "joy" is really only temporary relief from the pain they experience. Joy and suffering do not go together. Yet some people who have experienced great agony have been joyful because something greater than their suffering was present. Many of the great saints—Francis of Assisi, Teresa of Avila,

Real joy always wants to share.

—The Genesee Diary

John of the Cross—understood that human suffering allowed them to grow closer to Christ's suffering on the cross. So suffering and joy are not necessarily in tension. God's grace brings our human pain home to the place where God's joy resides so that we can know God's joy no matter what is going on in our lives. This is the gift of love: "May my joy be in you, and may your joy be complete" (see John 15:11).

The spiritual life, life with God in God's anguish, is about staying in touch with the love that becomes joy in us. It is so important to know that place and stay in touch with that joy so that it can be a stable undergirding for all our experiences. Belonging to Christ in the heart, where suffering and joy are no longer opposites, we share his victory over the world (John 15:19; 16:33).

OUR RESPONSE TO CHRIST'S JOY

How do we live out the joy Christ offers us? Celebration! This is the touchstone of joyful living. We need to learn to celebrate life. The church celebrates holy days like Christmas and Easter, and we celebrate birthdays, anniversaries, and special memorial days. But beyond these occasional celebrations, we are invited to develop an ongoing awareness that every moment is special and deserves to be recognized as a gift from the God with whom we share a home. To celebrate in this sense means to lift up our day, saying, "This is the day that the LORD has made; let us rejoice and be glad in it" (Ps. 118:24, NRSV).

The Promise

Everything that belongs to
Jesus is given for us
to receive.

—*Making All Things New*

Know that I am with you always.

—Matthew 28:20, JB

FOLLOWING JESUS does not mean holding in our imagination the memory of someone who lived two thousand years ago and trying to apply his teachings to our times. No, following Jesus means following the risen Lord, who is with us at this moment, drawing us more fully home into ever deepening communion with God.

"I am with you always; yes, to the end of time" (Matt. 28:20). That is the promise. Who is God? What is God's name? The first time God reveals this name is in the encounter with Moses at the burning bush. The name of God is "I AM" (Exodus 3:14). God is the God of Abraham, Isaac, and Jacob. When God is revealed to the people, they know God as the God *with* them. God is the one who comes to the people—to *us*, stays with us, journeys with us through the desert, and helps us find new life. In Jesus, we see how serious God is about being with us. God became one of us. There is nothing human that God has not shared with us.

There is, however, an even more profound way of God's being with us. Jesus says to us, "It is good for you that I leave, because when I leave I can send my spirit and my spirit will be able to dwell in you" (see John 16:7). Jesus reveals that God wants to be with us in a way so intimate that we can say God dwells *in* us. God-with-us is not only the God who travels with us, not only the God who suffers with us, but also the God who is the very breath by which we breathe. "I will be with you always, until the end of time." You and I are called to be living manifestations of God's glory in this world. That is the great promise—the promise of the Spirit.

Before the sending of the Spirit, the disciples traveled *with* Christ. After the sending of the Spirit, as they began to understand all that he had said to them, they traveled *in* Christ. When the disciples realized that Christ was living in them and they were living in him, when they could say, "Not I live, but Christ lives in me" (see Gal. 2:20), then all the boundaries broke open and they went out across the world. Christ with us as we are sent out into the whole world means that we can be anywhere and everywhere and still remain at home because we are already in communion with God. We are already dwelling in the house of the Lord. We do not need to be limited to one family, one community, one set of circumstances. We can be free simply to *be*, wherever we are sent.

The spiritual life is the place of true freedom.

—¡Gracias!

The art of spiritual living is to pay attention to the breathing of the Spirit right where we are and to trust that the Spirit is breathing new life in us now. The beauty of the spiritual life is that we can be where we are. We don't have to be any-where else. We are already home. So let's be there.

PRACTICING THE PRESENCE OF GOD

We practice the presence of God through prayer and service. Prayer is the way we become present to the moment and listen to God, who is always where we are. Prayer is the discipline of attentiveness, of being there with God. It is not necessary to have many words or deep thoughts or particular ways of thinking—just be in God's presence and say, "Lord, here I am . . . I love you . . . I know you love me . . . I want to be with you and I want you to be with me." Prayer is that simple.

Distractions in prayer usually mean we have left the present for the past or the future. We begin thinking about things that happened yesterday or worrying about things that might happen tomorrow. Distractions mean we are not fully present yet, and we can smile and accept this. But it is important to try to be more fully in the present because we know that God is here now. Prayer is being with God in the present.

Service is any small act of the kingdom through which we reach out to others with expressions of care. When we pray regularly and know that God is in us here and now, we are less preoccupied with ourselves and more attentive to others. Having left "me" to follow Jesus, we can see people with new clarity—their struggles, their beauty, their kindness. The Spirit in us sees the Spirit in them. There is a mutu-

It is in God that we find our neighbors and discover our responsibility to them.

—The Living Reminder

ality of the Spirit seeing the Spirit, of God praising God in acts of service for others. Therefore we can say that it is good for us to be with those we serve because they are living reminders of God's love.

As this recognition develops, community begins to form and new life begins to appear. Our acts of service become acts of gratitude undertaken to express thanks for the love we have experienced in God's coming to us, dwelling in us, inviting us home, and giving us eternal life. Gratitude allows us to be free of the need to change this person or that situation, and free for changes that may result from our actions—free indeed to care for the neighbor, the people of God, and the world.

Hidden Work

I can dwell in the house
of God and still be at home
in the houses of people.

—*Beyond the Mirror*

I am telling you the truth: it is for your
own good that I am going, because unless I go,
the Paraclete will not come to you; but if I go,
I will send him to you.

—John 16:7

J ESUS LEFT us so that we could live his own
life and form a new community of prayer and
service. Jesus says, "It is good for you that I leave,
because only when I leave will you come to
know fully who I am" (see John 16:7-14). Dear
friends, that is also true for this book. It's good
that it comes to an end. Perhaps what you have
read here and experienced through these pages
will become fruitful only later in your life. The
Spirit works deep in the heart, and you might
not be aware of this work right now. So let's wait
for the Spirit to be revealed more fully to us,
teaching us how to be at home in God's home,
and calling us to new forms of community and
new acts of service.

"Come, follow me."

(Matthew 19:21)

NOTES

1. Henri J. M. Nouwen, *The Road to Daybreak* (New York: Doubleday, 1988), 4.

2. Adapted from an unpublished Ash Wednesday meditation given on February 23, 1977 with additional material from a meditation on Psalm 46:10 given on November 7, 1979. The main text is drawn from archival taped recordings of meditations Henri Nouwen gave at St. Paul's Roman Catholic Parish, Harvard Square, during Lent 1985.

3. Cited in Sergius Bolshakoff, *Russian Mystics* (Kalamazoo, Mich.: Cistercian Publications, Inc., 1977), 253.

4. Martin Luther King Jr., *Strength to Love* (Philadelphia: Fortress Press, 1981), 54.

HENRI J. M. NOUWEN'S WORKS CITED

Page 12: *With Open Hands* (2006), 39.

Page 13: *The Way of the Heart* (1981), 77–78.

Page 15: *Can You Drink the Cup?* (2006), 112.

Page 18: *The Road to Daybreak* (1998), 68.

Page 21: *Lifesigns* (1986), 39.

Page 22: *Compassion* (2005), 27.

Page 25: *Finding Our Sacred Center* (2011), 14.

Page 26: *The Inner Voice of Love* (1996), 50.

Page 29: *Behold the Beauty of the Lord* (1987), 45.

Page 30: *Intimacy* (1969), 32.

Page 33: *The Road to Daybreak* (1998), 89.

Page 34: *Letters to Marc About Jesus* (1988), 60.

Page 36: *The Inner Voice of Love* (1996), 114.

Page 38: *The Wounded Healer* (1972), 87.

Page 41: *A Cry for Mercy* (1981), 78.

Page 44: *Jesus and Mary* (1993), 17.

Page 47: *Here and Now* (1994), 26.

Page 48: *The Genesee Diary* (1976), 180.

Page 51: *Making All Things New* (1981), 51.

Page 54: *¡Gracias!* (1983), 133.

Page 56: *The Living Reminder* (1977), 31.

Page 57: *Beyond the Mirror* (1990), 60.

ABOUT HENRI J. M. NOUWEN

Mary Ellen Kronstein

Henri Nouwen and John Mogabgab at Notre Dame in 1978

INTERNATIONALLY RENOWNED author, respected professor, and beloved pastor, Henri Nouwen wrote over forty books on the spiritual life that have inspired and comforted countless people throughout the world. Since his death in 1996, an ever-increasing number of readers, writers, and researchers are exploring his literary legacy. Henri Nouwen's works have been translated and published in more than twenty-two different languages.

Born in Nijkerk, Holland on January 24, 1932, Nouwen was ordained in 1957. Moved by his desire for a better understanding of human suffering, he went in 1964 to the United States to study in the Religion and Psychiatry Program at the Menninger Clinic. He went on to teach at the University of Notre Dame, the Pastoral Institute in Amsterdam, and the Divinity Schools of both Yale and Harvard, where his classes were among the most popular on campus.

His strong appeal as a teacher and writer had much to do with his passion to integrate all aspects of his life into a lived spirituality. Nouwen was convinced that striving for such integration is an urgent need in our culture. His writing, often autobiographical, has given readers a window into the joys and struggles of their own spiritual quest. The universal character of Nouwen's spiritual vision has crossed many boundaries and inspired a wide range of individuals: Wall Street bankers, politicians and professionals, Peruvian peasants, teachers, religious leaders, ministers and caregivers.

Nouwen traveled widely during his lifetime, lecturing on topics such as ministry and caregiving, compassion, peacemaking, suffering, solitude, community, dying, and death.

Nouwen was always searching for new images to convey the depth of the good news of the gospel message. For example, Henri met and befriended a group of trapeze artists in a travelling circus. Just prior to his sudden death, he was working on a project to use life in the circus as an image of the spiritual journey. *The Return of the Prodigal Son*, one of his classic works, marries art and spirituality in a contemporary interpretation of the ancient gospel parable.

Henri lived the last ten years of his life with people who have developmental disabilities in a L'Arche community near Toronto, Canada.

Inspired by Henri Nouwen's conviction that one's personal relationship with God is the foundation for all other relationships, the Henri Nouwen Society exists to create opportunities and resources that support people in their desire to grow spiritually.